HOME AGAIN!

OR,

THE LIEUTENANT'S DAUGHTERS.

A DOMESTIC DRAMA.

IN

Three Acts.

By EDWARD FITZBALL, Esq.

Author of Paul Clifford, The Siege of Rochelle, Madelaine, The Note Forger, Diadeste, Jonathan Bradford, &c.

THE ONLY EDITION CORRECTLY MARKED, BY PERMISSION, FROM THE PROMPTER'S BOOK.

To which is added,

A DESCRIPTION OF THE COSTUME - CAST OF THE CHARACTERS
THE WHOLE OF THE STAGE BUSINESS,
SITUATIONS—ENTRANCES—EXITS---PROPERTIES, AND
DIRECTIONS.

AS PERFORMED AT THE
London Theatres.

LONDON :
SAMUEL FRENCH,
PUBLISHER,
89, STRAND.

NEW YORK:
SAMUEL FRENCH & SON,
PUBLISHERS,
122, NASSAU STREET.

DRAMATIS PERSONÆ.

Squire Dillon	Mr. F. Vining
Lieutenant Leslie, R.N.	Mr. F. Matthews
Ben Bradshaw, a Young Agriculturist	Mr. Keeley
Charles Bradshaw, his Brother	Mr. Craven
Sheriff's Officer	Mr. Gough
Goaler	Mr. Silver

Alice Leslie .. ⎰ *The Lieutenant's* ⎱ .. Miss Fortescue
Sophy Leslie .. ⎱   *Daughters.*   ⎰ .. Mrs. Keeley

Servants, &c.

SCENE—Overhampton and London,

———

First produced at the Lyceum Theatre. November, 1844.
Time in Representation—1 hour 30 minutes.

———

COSTUME.

Dillon—Blue Newmarket coat, white waistcoat, coloured stock, grey trousers, boots, hat. Second dress. Rather shabby, slouched hat.

Lieutenant Leslie—Dark blue frock coat, white waistcoat, black stock, dark blue trousers, boots, grey wig. Second dress, Plain morning gown.

Ben—Bottle green coat, coloured waistcoat, white cord breeches, top boots and white hat. Second dress. Chesterfield coat, black hat, coloured silk handkerchief round throat.

Charles—Modern morning suit. Second dress. White Chesterfield.

Sheriff's Officer—Plain suit and black hat.

Gaoler—Coat, waistcoat, breeches, shoes.

Servants—White and scarlet liberies.

Alice—White muslin morning dress. Second dress. Pelisse and bonnet. Third dress. Plain grey stuff. Fourth dress. The same as the First.

Sophy—Plain muslin morning dress. Second dress. Bonnet and shawl, Third dress, Plain brown stuff, Fourth dress. The same as the first.

ARTICLES NEEDED BY AMATEURS.

MAGNESIUM TABLEAUX LIGHTS.

A metal capable of being ignited by a common match, and burning with great brilliancy, producing a light that can be seen thirty miles. Unequalled in beauty and brilliancy. This is the best light for moonlight and statuary. It is so intense that it causes gas-light to cast a shadow. Price each package, ... 1 0

PREPARED BURNT CORK

For Negro Minstrels. This article we can recommend as it can be taken off as easily as put on. In which it differs from most all others manufactured. In tin boxes enough for 50 performances. Price per box 1 0

SPIRIT GUM.

The best in use, prepared expressly for securing the Moustachios, Whiskers, Crape, Hair, &c., &c. Will adhere strongly in the hottest weather. Price 1s. 0d. per bottle. Can only be sent by Carrier.

PREPARED WHITING.

For Pantomimes, Clowns' faces, Statuary, &c. This is not affected by per-spiration. Price per box 1 0

MONGOLIAN

Is a paste, for Indians, Mulattoes, &c. One Shilling.

LIGHTNING FOR PRIVATE THEATRICALS.

Box containing the necessary material and full instructions for producing the same without danger. Per Box, One Shilling and Sixpence.

FRENCH'S SCENES FOR AMATEURS.

From approved designs. Representing scenes suitable for any piece. These are in-valuable to amateur scene painters and also a great guide and help to professionals. Price Coloured, each, One Shilling. Plain, each, Sixpence.

1. Cottage, Interior	6. Castle	11. Street, Foreign
2. „ Exterior	7. Street	12. Roadside Inn with river
3. Wood	8. Palace	and bridge
4. Prison	9. Drawing-room	
5. Field	10. Library	

THEATRICAL FACE PREPARATIONS.

We would call the attention of our customers to the fact that all the preparations here advertised are the best manufactured; they are all imported by us direct from Paris, and they are guaranteed to be perfectly harmless. They are all ready to use.

	s.	d.
Rouge for the Theatre, in neat box, each No. 1...	1	0
Rouge, very fine „ „ No. 2	1	0
Rouge, finest quality made from flowers, perfumed, No. 3	1	6

It is absolutely necessary to use some rouge when acting, for a face without it looks perfectly white. This effect is produced by the foot and side lights.

	s.	d.
White for the Theatre (Blanc de Perle) same as Rouge No. 1	1	0
„ „ „	1	0
„ „ „	1	6

This is used principally for the hands and arms, and also to heighten the effect of the Rouge on the face. In plays where sickness or fainting to be re-presented this is indispensable.

	s.	d.
Pencils for the eye-lids and eye-brows	1	0
Pencils for the veins (Crayons d'Italie)	1	0
Grenadine for the lips, gives them a fine colour and improves the entire countenance	1	6
Tablettes de Jouvence, a small box of rouge or white	1	0
Boxes of Blue for Veins, with estamp used in putting it on, a superior article	3	0
Fard Indien, used for eyebrows and eye-lids, very effective	3	0
Etui Mysterieux (Mysterious Box) contains Crayons à Sourciels, Houppe, Rouge, Blanc, &c.	3	0

Boxes of powder for the Hair. In neat boxes all ready to use, enough for several occasions. Indispensable in plays of the 16th, 17th and 18th centuries.

	s.	d.
Gold	2	0
Silver	2	0
Diamond	2	0

See Catalogues (sent free) for complete list of Amateur Articles.

HOME AGAIN.

ACT 1.

SCENE I.—*The Briary Cottage*, R. H. *A low paling, with stile, at back,* L. H., *surrounds a garden, filled with roses. The high road, and village in the distance. Daybreak.*

Enter Alice *and* Sophy *from the cottage, arm in arm.*
[*The clock strikes Seven as the Curtain rises*]

Sophy (*a basket of flowers on her arm*). Seven, by the church clock, Alice. In half an hour Charles Bradshaw will leave Overhampton for London.

Alice (*sighing*). For London? For India, Sophy—which, you know, is much further, and a much more dangerous distance.

Sophy. I'm sorry he's going, ain't *you*, Alice.

Alice (*sighing*). Yes. He's a very nice young man.

Sophy. Very! and nice young men are so scarce—especially in Overhampton. Then we've known Charles ever since we were children, no taller than that geranium. We shall miss him when he's gone, shan't we Alice? If it had been his brother Ben, now, his loss would have been no great matter. Ben is so very simple and ridiculous, [*Laughing.*]

Alice, True—he is, as you say, simple-minded, but then Ben Bradshaw is ever ready to do a kindness to anyone—run your errands, hold your silk, tie up your roses, and in short, he's——

Sophy. To sum it correctly up—more useful than ornamental. But then he shews some taste by being so in love with you, Alice.

Alice (*patting her on cheek*). Jealous pate! Don't you think it's your pretty little own self that poor Ben sighs for ?

Sophy. Ha, ha, ha! Well I must say he's a love of a fright. But he'll sigh a long time, if I should happen to go for to prove the fortunate object of his adoration—although, to tell you the truth, Alice, I don't think the poor fellow knows exactly which of us two it is he intends the honour of becoming Mrs. B. Ha. ha, ha! [*Gathers roses*, R. H, *Coach horn heard without,* U. E. L. H.]

Alice. [*Excitedly.*] There's the coach! Charles promised to come and bid us farewell.

Sophy. Did he! It was very kind; I hope he'll not forget to keep his word. Young men are so apt to do that.

Alice. [*With emotion.*] I almost wish he might, for it is very painful to say good bye.

Sophy. So it is. Why, Alice, you are crying. What's the matter?

Alice. [*Evasively*] O—h! I ran a thorn into my finger!

Sophy. Did you? It doesn't bleed! Let me look! Ah, here is Charles Bradshaw!

Enter CHARLES BRADSHAW, *through gate, equipped for travelling. He comes down* C.

Charles. Dear Miss Leslie's—I am here to take my leave of you. I fear, for a long time. [Sophy, R. Charles, C. Alice, L.]

Alice. [*Agitated*] You are then really going to India, Mr. Charles? I wish you——[*Bursts into tears.*]

Sophy. [*Apart—observing her tears.*] That thorn must be a very sharp one'

Charles. [*With effort.*] Dear Miss Leslie. only a few moments are left me to declare what I have never yet had the courage to utter—I——[*Irresolutely*] My voyage to India is entirely on your account.

Alice. My account!

Charles. Yes—that I may be enabled to offer you an independency worthy of—that is, forgive me—I mean to make——

Sophy. [*Surprised.*] A declaration! [*Apart.*] I know!

Alice. [*Remonstrating*] Sophy!

Charles. Yes—thank you, Miss Sophy, kindly—a declaration. That is it. An offer of my heart and hand before I set out. We have known each other long,—and—and I have—have always thought—that is—I have always hoped —Alice——

Alice [*Confused.*] Charles! [*Coach horn again heard.*

Sophy. [C.] What nonsense to stand shilly shally that way. and the coach within a hundred yards of the door! You love one another—every body knows that, except Ben Bradshaw, and why can't you say so?

Alce. Sophy. this jesting——

Charles. Believe me, dear Miss Leslie. Sophy is not jesting. The time is indeed precious—at least to me. **Do** allow me to clasp on your arm this gold bracelet—it will serve to remind you of me when I am far, far away! [*Clasping bracelet, and kissing her hand.*]

Sophy. [*Apart—peeping.*] A bracelet! It's very nice to have a young man in love with you. [*As he kisses* Alice's *hand.*] Oh! [*Affecting to conceal her face.* BEN BRADSHAW *appears at top,* L. H. *on stile.*]

Ben. [*On stile.*] Come, I say, Charles—what are you about? The coach is going to hop off from the "Jolly Cock Sparrows"—you'll lose your place!

Charles. Heaven bless you, Alice! You'll not forget me?

Alice. No. Charles—never!

Charles. [*Going.*] Adieu, Miss Sophy!

Sophy. [*Putting down her basket,* R. H.] Stay a moment. I wish to place this rose in your button hole.

Ben. Hem! She never wishes to place a rose in my button-hole! [*Crossing behind to* R. H.] Now her back is turned, I'll pop my love letter into her basket! [*Drops letter, sighing.*] I'm sure my face must be as red as them hollyhocks!

Sophy. [*Turning.*] Mr. Bradshaw! What are you doing with my flower basket?

Ben. [*Stammering. Apart.*] I nearly put my foot in it! I thought perhaps, Miss Sophy, as you were so generous this morning, fastening roses in young men's button-holes, you might find a stray daffydowndilly to place in mine. [*Coach horn heard.*]

Charles [*Pulling him.*] Come, come—some other time, Ben—or I shall be indeed too late. Once more—Heaven bless you, Miss Leslie! Excuse me, Sophy—I——[Charles *hurries out through* L. H.]

Ben. To Sophy.] Don't fret! I shall see you again about breakfast time. [*Seeing* Sophy *at basket.*] If I can muster courage——[Sophy *takes up basket.*]—Oh, la! I hope she won't find the letter till I'm gone? [*Falls over stile.* Oh!

Sophy. [*Laughs.* Ha, ha, ha!

Alice. For shame, Sophy! [*Smiles through her tears.*]

LIEUTENANT LESLIE *appears at window,* R. H.

Lieut. Girls, is breakfast ready?

Sophy. Yes, dear pa—we are only waiting for you.

Lieut. I shall be down immediately. [*Shuts the window.*]

Alice. And the tea not made! [*Exit into house,* R. H. *drying her eyes.*]

Sophy. [*Looking over stile.*] Ah, there goes the coach up

the hill. Now it turns the corner ! There it is, again—no,
it isn't ! Good bye ! Only think—Alice has got a sweet-
heart ! a real *earnest* one. La ! I wish somebody would
make me an offer. 'Tis so pretty—so amusing ! A dashing
young soldier—or a sailor ! I should prefer a sailor, because Pa's a sailor. Ha. ha! [*Sings.*]

> He's on the sea ! he's on the sea !
> His light barque bounding on the wind—
> Each wild wave bears him still from me,
> And leaves me weeping far behind.
> He's on the sea, &c.

[*During the Air she gathers more flowers, places them
in her basket, then places the basket on her head, and trips
into the cottage, singing.*]

———

SCENE II.—*The High Road, near the Briary.*

Enter DILLON, R. H.

Dil. So—that plodding fool, Charles Bradshaw. is gone—
I trust, for ever. His visible regard for Alice Leslie, in
particular, rendered him a most detestable object in my
eyes. I have now no longer a rival to dread.

Enter BEN, R. H.

Ben. There they go ! [*Looking,* L. H,] Good bye !
good——[*Runs against* Dillon.]

Dil. What, the devil——Oh, it's you, is it. Mr. Ben
Bradshaw ? Coming from the Briary, as usual. Always
fussing and flirting with those girls. For a fellow with no
head, I must think you are rather cunning:

Ben. Come, I say—none of that. I'm not responsible
for my comings and goings to you, you know, Mr. Dillon.

Dil. You have no right to haunt that house the way you
do, without coming to a declaration.

Ben. Declaration ! What's that ?

Dil. Bah ! A proposal of marriage. I suppose you
have the conceit to be in love with one of them.

Ben. Well, suppose I have — is that any affair of yours ?
I like that ! Conceit, you said ? Do you happen to know,
sir, that my grandfather's property—four thousand pounds
—has come to me, as heir at law ? Mr. Dillon, that gives
me a title, and makes me a gentleman, doesn't it ? And
though I say it, either of the Miss Leslie's might catch a
worse partner for life.

Dil. [*With sarcasm*] Where ?

Ben Yourself, for instance !

Dil. [*Angrily*] How ?

Ben. Oh, I can't tell how. Though you be Squire Dillon,

you arn't every woman's picking and choosing—and may be, by the time you leave of horse-racing, gambling, and all that sort of thing, I may be as rich as you, you know. [*Crosses to* R. H.]

Dil. What is the idiot raving about? You surely do not, cannot mean to insinuate that one or t'other of those girls could possibly look upon such an insect as you in any other light than as a mere laughing-stock?

Ben. [*Offended.*] Insect! I'm no caterpillar!

Dil. Then what do you do creeping and crawling about that house? Pray which of the Miss Leslie's is it you honour with your especial favour and regard, eh, dolt? Is it Alice?

Ben. Hem! I suppose you think you are talking to your hounds. But I can tell you. Mister Squire, I wasn't born in a wood to be scared by an owl—he, he!

Dil. I tell you what, Mr. Bradshaw—Old Leslie seems disposed to go back from his word with me, as regards one of his daughters—I suppose you, you pitiful clodhopper, and your paltry four thousand pounds, have come in his way.

Ben. Oh, my! Do you call four thousand pounds paltry?

Dil. Yes—it must be so, and I insist on immediately receiving——

Ben. What? my four thousand——

Dil. Bah! An immediate explanation. I will not be trifled with—I will not, by——

Ben. Well, then—since you insist on an explanation—mind, you insist—I'll tell you. If you've made up your mind to Alice Leslie, it's no go!

Dil. [*Violently.*] Is it yourself who is beforehand with me?

Ben. Oh, I don't say that, There are other good-looking young men besides me, and other ill-favoured one's besides you. That's comfort for you! And if you want to know particulars, you had better go to the Briary, and ask Mr. Leslie—only beware of the spring guns and steel traps, that's all—he, he! [*Exit* L. H.

Dil. Imbecile But he is too contemptible for my rage. The old Lieutenant is in my debt—deeply in my debt! I've entangled him in every way—still he affects coldness as to my passion for Alice—and she also turns a deaf ear to my love. But I will possess her, I'm determined—and that shortly, or she and her proud poverty-struck family shall feel how easy it is to lift the head above our betters, and how difficult to keep it in that position. I'll to my

lawyer's—then to demand of this insolent Lieutenant payment, or the daughter's hand—the daughter's hand !

[*Exit* L. H.

— —

SCENE III.—*Tee Breakfast Parlour in the Briary.   Windows looking on to lawn   Breakfast table set.   Easy
chair, Piano, Bust of Shakspeare, Chairs, &c.:*

ALICE *discovered* R H. *putting toast on table.* SOPHY
seated L. H. *reading a letter, and laughing.*

Alice. Why what letter is that which makes you laugh so,
Sophy ?

Sophy. A love letter, Alice

Alice, A love letter '

Sophy. Yes—a proposal.   I found it in my basket, where
it must have been left last night, I think.

Alice. Last night ? Nobody called, save a boy at the gate
with images, and Ben Bradshaw.

Sophy. You've hit it—Ben Bradshaw is the real Simon
Pure.   But listen, and subdue your envy. [*Reads*] "My
dear Miss Sophy—I dream of you day and night—in
short, I can't rest for thinking of you. I love you better
than I do my mother. Now you know the worst, Dear
Miss Sophy—I shall call in during the morning, if it don't
rain. Please to put me out of my misery at once. I would
as soon have faced a loaded cannon as have told all this to
your face.   So no more at present— only believe me, your
loving lover, BEN BRADSHAW." P. S.—Mother says, if
you want a little sweetwort, she brews to-morrow." [*Sophy laughs.*]

Alice. [*Laughing. Gets kettle, ana pours water into tea
pot, &c.*] Ha, ha, ha ! Poor Ben ! Of course you mean
to accept ?

Sophy. Certainly.   Who could resist the sweetwort ? but,
hush—here's father. [*They both laugh.*]

Enter LIEUTENANT LESLIE. L. H.

Lieut. Well, my girls—I'm glad to find you in such excellent spirits.   Ah ! it's all the effects of early rising, and
the fine air of the garden. Is the newspaper come ? [*Alice
pours out tea, &c.*]

Sophy. Here it is, father—[*Getting it from off piano.*]—
and full of births, marriages, and such a deal of ship news.

Lieut. [*Seating himself.*] I'm glad of that. It's beautiful
weather ! [*Reads.*] " Arrived from New York." Ah, nothing but steam now. The kettle's boiling over, Alice—
and Charles Bradshaw, he's off for—for—[*Reads.*]—Table Land ! eh ?

Alice. No, Pa—for Calcutta !

Lieut. (*reading*). " Cutter !" No, no—brig.

Alice. Charles Bradshaw is gone to his uncle's, at Calcutta.

Lieut. True, true—and a stingy old hunks his uncle is. A nabob—though wealthy as—By the bye—while I was shaving at the window, I saw that simpleton, Ben Bradshaw, crossing the Common. [*Double knock at* L. H. D.] That's his knock ! He always imitates the twopenny postman, by way of being genteel. Come in ! Sophy, dear—why don't you run and let him in ?

Sophy (*confused*). I, Papa !

Alice. I'll do it. [*Opens door,* U. E. L. H., Ben *enters awkwardly.*]

Ben (*nodding at door sheepishly*), Ah, how do ye do ?

Lieut. How do *you* do ? Come in and sit down. [Ben *comes forward.*] Just in time for the hot rolls. Why don't one of you take Mr. Bradshaw's hat? You see he doesn't know what to do with it.

Sophy (*taking hat—putting it on, and surveying herself at glass,* R. H. *over piano.*) What a very dashing hat this is, Mr. Bradshaw. I don't wonder at your making so many conquests.

Ben (*sheepishly*). Come, I say—none of that you know, Miss Sophy. [*Taking away hat, and putting it before him.*]

Alice. There's a chair, Mr. Bradshaw——[*Points* L. H. *at top.*]

Ben (*shuffling about*). Thank you, miss. I was just going to observe——There's a fly fallen into the cream, and—eh ?

Lieut. Why what the devil's the matter with the fellow? Slew yourself to an anchor, do ! [*Pulls him on seat he lets down his hat—Sophy picks it up, and puts it on the bust.*]

Alice. Sugar, Mr. Bradshaw?

Ben. Soft, if you please—I always take it soft. Ugh! [*Putting his fingers to his mouth.*]

Alice (*pouring out hot water*). Oh, I beg your pardon. I didn't notice your fingers in the slop basin.

Sophy (*with affected sympathy*). I hope you are not scalded, Mr. Bradshaw? Shall I apply anything to your hand ?

Ben. No, I thank you, ma—am ! It's very well, I thank you. How do you find yourself? You are likely to produce a very fine crop of potatoes this year, I think, if one may judge by appearances.

Lieut Then you came through the kitchen garden, I suppose?

Ben. I didn't like to come in at the front gate—I was so abashed.

Lieut. Abashed! Abashed at what?

Alice. Roll, Mr. Bradshaw?

Sophy. Cream, Mr. Bradshaw? [*They help him.*]

Ben. [*Speaking with his mouth full.*] Thank you, I——

Lieut. Why don't you let him answer me? Deuce take it! Why you've spilt the tea all over my dressing gown!

Ben. I beg pardon, I——[*Upsets chair.*]

Lieut. Never mind—I'll change it in an instant. There —there—no fuss—no fuss! I hate fuss' [*Exit L. H.*

Sophy. Now, Mr. Bradshaw—as I and Alice have no secrets—to put you out of your misery—[*Curtsies.*]—I'm engaged! [*Aside.*] At least, I hope to be!

Ben. La! Engaged! Well, if mother didn't say one of you was engaged. It's *you*, is it? I've made a mistake, then.

Sophy. A mistake!

Ben. Yes—it's Alice—[*Crosses to* C.]—that I ought to be in love with! Mother said I should make some confounded blunder, when she threw the old slipper after me for good luck, as I left home.

Alice [*Smiling.*] It's very kind of you, Mr. Bradshaw— but, to put you out of your misery again, I'm engaged also.

Ben. Ah, I remember—to Mr. Dillon!

Alice To Mr. Dillon! I!

Ben. Yes. Oh, bless you—he told me all about it. He said he should be here this morning.

Lieut. [*Without.*] But let me tell you, sir——

Dil. [*Without.*] Well, sir—hear me!

Ben. He's proposing to your father now, I've no doubt.

Enter LIEUTENANT, L. H. D *followed by* DILLON, *angrily.*

Lieut. I must beg, Mr. Dillon, that you will not think of intruding upon me in my own house.

Dil. [*Putting down his hat and cane on chair* L. *of table. Bitterly.*] Your house, sir Mine, if you please.

Lieut. Yours, as far as inheritance goes—but mine, while I pay rent for it.

Dil. Yes—when that rent is paid. At present——

Lieut. At present, nor at any time will I calmly submi

to insult—therefore, begone, sir, or I must be at the un-
pleasant trouble of turning you out.

Dil. [*Enraged.*] You turn me out, Leslie! You have
said it! Look to yourself! I have said it! I came hither
with every honourable intention of urging my claim to
your daughter's hand—the hand of Alice.

Alice. [*Comes down,* R, H.] Claim my hand, Mr. Dillon!

Dil. Yes. You know well enough of my love, Alice,
though, like your arrogant father, your pride leads you to
affect not to understand me. But it resolves itself into this
one question—am I, or am I not to be considered by you
in the light of an accepted suitor?

Alice. I have told you before, sir, that I have no desire
to change—that is, to leave my father.

Dil. In short, that——

Lieut. She cannot love you. I have assured you of that
already.

Dil. Very well, sir—very well, *Mister* Leslie. Your
servant, *Miss* Leslie. Your father just now ordered me out
of the house. Me, the man you find it impossible to love.
Remember—*I* shall not forget!

Sophy. [*Smoothing his hat, and coming down on his*
R H.] Here's your hat, Mr. Dillon——[*He does not take
it.*]

Ben. [*Coming down on his* L. H.] And your stick, Mr.
Dillon——

Dil. Idiot! [*Striking him with it.*]

Ben. Oh! [*Seizing him by the collar, and taking stick
from him.*] I say, none of that, though, if you please.
Though I may not be quite as wise as you are, maybe I'm
as courageous, and as strong, too, if you come to that—so
out with you! You gave the first offence, so away with
you! [*Forces him off at door, then goes to window.*]
There's your hat—when your head's cool, put it on—and
your stick! If you meet with a mad bull, or anything
more furious than yourself, knock it down, since you are so
fond of knocking! [*Throws them out, and shuts window.*]

Dil. [*Without.*] Reptile I'll——But, no matter! [*At
window—threatening.*] Revenge—revenge! [Dillon *disap-
pears.*]

Ben. and Sophy. Ha, ha, ha, ha!

Lieut. Silence, Sophy—your mirth seriously offends me.

Sophy. [L. C.] I can't help laughing at the ridiculous
figure Dillon cut, when Ben whisked him out of the door!

Lieut. It was a very great liberty on the part of Mr.
Bradshaw in another man's house!

Ben. [L.] Didn't he affront you, by——

Lieut. I thank you, sir—but Lieutenant Leslie knows how to resent an insult offered to himself without the assistance of another.

Sophy. But father, Dillon struck Mr. Bradshaw.

Lieut. He should have resented the affront, then, somewhere else—at least, it was injudicious here, and before ladies: [*Goes up* R. H. *with* Alice.]

Ben. Pooh   I couldn't help it—my blood was up. And just feel, Miss Sophy—here's a bump from the knob of his cane, as big as that hard boiled egg !

Sophy. Shall I put some vinegar and brown paper upon it, Mr. Bradshaw ?

Ben. [*Feeling the bump, and tying his handkerchief over it*] I owe Dillon a grudge !   I'll go and swear my life against him—I will !   Lord ! why if my head hadn't been as thick as a trencher, he might have knocked out my brains.   Only think !   I ain't a malicious man, nor an obstinate man—but a blow's a blow, and a bump's a bump— [*Crosses to* R.]—and when one feels it throbbing and smarting, as I do, he just puts on——[*Taking* Sophy's *bonnet.*]

Sophy. Not my bonnet, if you please, Mr. Bradshaw. That's your hat on the bust of Shakespeare.

Ben. It's all the same !   [*Holding his head.*] Ugh ! My eye ! he shall pay for this. [*Crosses to* L. H. *flourishing stick.*]

Lieut. [*Up stage.*] Be calm, Mr. Bradshaw——

Ben. Calm !   Very likely.   Calm !   Fancy your nose between a pair of nut-crackers—fancy—[*Unlocking door*] —Ugh ! Now I've nearly nipped off my thumb !   He shall pay for it ! [*Goes—returns,*] Oh, I beg pardon—I forgot my manners—but he shall pay for it !   [*Exit* L. H. D.

Alice. Dear father, call him back—this will only lead to further misunderstanding.

Sophy. [*Looking out.*] Call him back ! Why he's already half across the common, capering like a wild donkey !

Lieut. Let him go, girls.   His folly, and Dillon's rage will burn out as quickly as a straw fire, depend on it. [*He sits at table.*] Let us now conclude our breakfast in peace. I heard you in excellent voice in the garden just now, Sophy.   Let me hear that song you were singing so sweetly, while Alice pours out the tea.

Sophy. Yes, dear pa ! [*Sits at piano.*]

BALLAD—SOPHY.

He's on the sea ! he's on the sea !
His light barque bounding through the wind—

Each white wave bears him still from me,
　　And leaves me weeping far behind.
My lute lies in my lattice lone,
　　Untun'd those chords so fraught with glee—
The music of my soul is gone,
　　He's on the sea! he's on the sea!

The perfum'd rose, the moonlit ray,
　　Sweet distant chime of village bell,
Their charms have faded all away—
　　He's gone, and they nave lost their spell.
I watch the wild birds hover round,
　　And wish thi sheart, like theirs, were free;
On wings of air to him I'd bound,
　　Far o'er the sea! far o'er the sea.

Lieut. Bravo, my little syren! But, Alice, what makes your hand tremble so? and you look as pale——

Alice. Dear father, I cannot forget Dillon's threat. You heard what he said. It was a frightful word—revenge!

Lieut. A word which——

Dil. (*bursting in* L. H. D. *followed by an* Officer). He means to keep! Officer, Lieutenant Leslie is your prisoner at my suit, unless he can immediately discharge the amount of——[*All rise.*]

Lieut. Villain. [*Comes down to* L. C.] You know I cannot. You know but too well the thing is impossible! Before my children, too—my poor girls—to wreak your malice thus! [*Proudly.*] But I am quite willing to go!

Alice R. *and Sophy* L., *clinging to him.*] No, father—no!

Lieut. Yes, my dears—there is no alternative. It is but a temporary inconvenience. In a day or two, doubtless, at furthest, I shall be at home—[*Apart*]—or never. I dare not trust myself to gaze upon them, lest that monster should exult in the tears his brutality wrings from the heart of an old lieutenant! [*Going.*]

Alice (*putting on her bonnet*). Dear father, do you think that we will remain here without you!

Sophy (*putting on her bonnet, and sobbing.*) No, no—father! [*Gets* L. H. *of him.*]

Lieut. Yes, yes—it is my wish—my command! Let them clap me under hatches where they will, I can endure it—but to see my poor girls, for whom I almost thought the breath of heaven too rough, the inmates of a place so vile as that to which I am going, it would kill me—it would kill me!

Alice. Oh, father—that place is [Lieutenant *hesitates.*]

Dil. To the county gaol, unless——

Alice. [L. C. *Proudly.*] Monster! I neither asked for your information, nor require conditions of lenity. This brutal outrage has cancelled all intercourse—all obligations between us—and the daughters of Lieutenant Leslie know too well their father's manly pride to wound it by any concession—even for his sake—to a ruffian like you!

Lieut. [*Pressing her hand, violently.*] Alice—my daughter—you have spoken the sentiments of your father's heart! I would rather perish in a dungeon—on straw—than sacrifice my child, or that he should think I am unmanned by his malice! Alice, give me my hat, You know me, girls! Be firm—no tears—not a step—not a word! Now, sir, I am at your service! [*Goes proudly out, followed by* Officer]

Dil. [*Smiling.*] Ladies, your servant——[*Exit, bowing.* Lieutenant *passes the window, casting at them a parting glance.* Dillon *follows, taking off his hat.*]

Sophy. Alice!

Alice. Sophy! [*They rush into each other's arms, weeping, as the Act Drop falls*]

END OF ACT I.

ACT II.

SCENE I.—*The Park Gates of Dillon House. Bank on* R. H. *Thunder, lightning, and rain. As the Scene opens, the storm is violent. Lights down.*

Enter ALICE, R. H. *supporting* SOPHY,

Alice. Dear Sophy, why this alarm? It is but a passing storm. Why terrify yourself and me? Here, under this friendly oak—or on this mossy bank, rest—rest! You are weary, and worn out with walking—and it is three long tedious miles to the county gaol.

Sophy. Oh, yes. And poor father ill—as his letter evidently betrayed—though he strove to conceal it. I am quite well again now, Alice—and see, the moon is rising! In an hour we can be at the place, and father will be so happy to see us. Now, Alice, now——[*They proceed—a flash of forked lightning through the trees terrifies* Sophy, *and she faints at the park gate. Storm.*] Sophy—dear Sophy—speak to me—your own sister! Alas, alas—I fear she's dead. Help, there—help, some one! [*Rings gate bell*] Help, for mercy's sake! No answer! Is the house deserted? Must she, then, perish for the want of aid? [*Joyfully.*] No—this way I hear a footstep! 'Tis—[DILLON *enters*, L. H.]—Dillon!

Dil. Alice Leslie! How am I indebted for this appeal at the gate of Dillon park?

Alice. Your house! Alas, in my affliction I knew it not, believe me!

Dil. What, then, is the matter, if I am not to understand——

Alice. On our way to—to visit our father, who is ill. Sophy, exhausted by excitement and the sudden coming on of the storm, fainted. I merely rang at that bell for assistance.

Dil. [*Apart.*] Thanks to the lucky star which has driven her to seek refuge here, thus forlorn—exhausted! [*With contrition.*] Oh, Alice—it is I fiend that I am—it is I who have reduced you to this—but believe me, Alice—believe me, the deep remorse which now tears this devoted heart might serve as some atonement, if balanced against the anguish which I have endured for your sake—heaven knows how long and keenly. But if you cannot forgive—at least let us together assist poor Sophy in.

Sophy. [*Rising terrified.*] No, no—go on, Alice—I am quite well now, or if I were not, I would sooner drop lifeless by the way, than enter his house!

Dil. Sophy—Alice—this is folly—madness! [*Storm.*] You cannot—must not attempt to proceed. Listen to the increasing fury of the tempest. Alice—I will comply with your every desire—only come into the house—your father shall be liberated in the morning—I promise, on the word of a——

Sophy. Pass the night beneath this roof! Never—never!

Alice. Now, Sophy—lean on me——

Dil. [*Crosses and interposes.*] You must not—shall not go!

Alice. [*Proudly.*] How, sir! Do you dare to stop us on the king's highway?

Enter Servants, *through gate,* c.

Ha! here are your servants. If you presume to interpose between us and our journey, I will appeal to them, even against their master! Let go my hand, Mr. Dillon! Alice Leslie the defenceless, as you behold her, is not to be insulted with impunity! Away, Sophy—away!

Sophy. Yes, dear Alice—our father expects—oh, Alice—support me—or—I——[*She is falling—*Dillon *runs and catches her in his arms—*Servants *enter from park with lights.*]

Dil. You see, Alice, 'tis quite impossible to proceed—the poor girl is dying!

Alice. Dying!

Dil. At least, without assistance. In my arms—mine—

I'll bear her in. Follow without fear—and, if you wish it, I swear to you that I wilt even quit the house till your departure. Come, Alice, follow !

[*Exit through gates, c. carrying Sophy.*

Alice. [*Troubled.*] What web is this which entangles me ! Sophy—my sister ! what will become of us !

[*Exi through gates, c. followed by* Servants.

SCENE II.—*A Room in the County Gaol. A door in F.*
R. H.

Enter LIEUTENANT LESLIE, L. H.

Lieut. Well—suppose this is the quarter-deck—suppose I am pacing up and down—mid watch—why not—why not ? Because there is liberty—sweet heaven-winged liberty—at stake, without which who could be happy ? My poor girls ! When despairingly I reflect that their father—their only friend and protector—may, too probably, end his wretched remnant of life in a prison—oh, the thought almost drives me mad—mad—mad ! [*Pacing to and fro.*]

Enter Gaoler, R D. F.

Gaoler. Lieutenant Leslie, you are free !

Lieut. Free ! I ! It must be a mistake. I have no friend, who either could, or would discharge my debts.

Enter BEN BRADSHAW, R. D. F. *His hat tied on with his handkerchief.*

Ben. [*Shakes hands.*] Oh, yes, but you have, though—Ben Bradshaw ! The man without a head, as I'm called at Overhampton. They shan't say I haven't a heart, though ! No, I'll take care of that. Lieutenant, there's your discharge. [*Gives paper.*]

Lieut. Amazement ! My dear Ben—I shall never be able to repay your generosity

Ben. Generosity ! None o' that ! Lord bless you ! I'm amply repaid in out-spiting that Mr. Dillon. Not that that alone is the purpose of my generosity, as you call it. No—I like you, Lieutenant—and, morover, I couldn't bear to see the two dear young ladies so miserable.

Lieut Ah, my girls ! Tell me—how are they ?

Ben. Both well—at mother's, on the Common. It's more lively than the Briary, now you are away. Something to see—such lots of donkeys and geese !

Lieut. At your mother's ? Ah, I comprehend—turned out of the Briary ! An execution, eh ?

Ben. Well, never mind. Let us lose no time. They'd

rather catch a sight of you, than all the old family chairs
and tables in Christendom !

Lieut. What an execrable scoundrel is that accursed
Dillon ! My girls without a home—without a home ! [*He
crosses* R. H.]

Ben. Not exactly—and when you arrive, all will be better than ever. Won't they be astonished ! I never said a
word about coming hither, or what I was going to do.
Won't Alice smile ? Won't the bright eyes of Sophy glit-
ter,? Come, Lieutenant—I have got my cob and whiskey
at the door. The brute doesn't tumble down above twice
in a mile, and we shall be at Overhampton before the muf-
fins are toasted, if you make haste.

Lieut. Come on, my friend—come on ! My children—
my dear children ! how my heart beats to feel myself once
more in your affectionate arms !   [*Exit* R. D. F.

Ben. [*Looking at a chalk sketch of a gallows on the
wall.*] Well, I never ! [*The door is closed.*] Hillo ! I
say—none of that, though, Mr. Turnkey.

Gaoler. Oh, I axes pardon—but you seemed struck with
the place, and I didn't wish to hurry you.

Ben. I thank you—but I am neither struck with your
residence nor your family portraits. There's a half crown
for you, to drink the Lieutenant's health, when I'm gone—
only do rub out that likeness of yourself—it isn't flatter-
ing !

Gaoler. Ha, ha, ha !   [*Exeunt* R. D. F.

———

SCENE III.—*An Elegant Apartment in Dillon Park.
Doors opening to a suite of costly chambers at back.
Tables, chairs, &c. Fire burning.*

Enter ALICE *and* SOPHY, *at back.* C. R.

Sophy. [*Looking about.*] Isn't this a lovely place,
Alice ? What elegant furniture ! Just peep into that costly
mirror - how beautifully it reflects your figure from head to
foot. [*Whispers.*] Oh, if all this splendour did but belong
to Charles Bradshaw instead of Mr. Dillon, wouldn't it be
a happiness to see you reign here as lady of the hall ?

Alice. [R.] Thank heaven, you appear perfectly re-
stored, Sophy. Do you think you are now well enough to
proceed ? I am all impatience to be gone. These splen-
dours only distress me, while I reflect that our poor father
remains the solitary inmate of a prison !

Sophy. That remark serves me as I deserve; but indeed, Alice, I had not forgotten. [*Weeps.*]

Alice. Nor had I the slightest intention of wounding your feelings, dear Sophy. [*Kisses her*] So do run and bring our shawls and bonnets. Dillon—who really has had the delicacy not to intrude upon us—appears not to be stirring, therefore the sooner we set forward on our journey again the better.

Sophy I shan't be a minute [*Crosses to* R. H.] How magnificently the sun shines in a' that window! It's a lovely morning, and we'll trip along the road as briskly as though we were going to your wedding, Alice. [*She runs out,* R. H.]

Alice. [*Sighing.*] My wedding! alas! But why am I so selfish as to waste a single sigh for the anguish of my own heart, when every moment chides any delay from my father I will instantly—[*Goes to* L. H.]—make my acknowledgements to the housekeeper. and—[*Going, encounters* Dillon *who enters at back.*] Dillon!

Dil. Why do you turn from me, Alice? Have you any cause to reproach me for want of hospitality while under this roof?

Alice No, no, Mr. Dillon—none! and I thank you most gratefully, for my poor sister's sake. But she is quite well now, and I was going to hasten her departure. [*Going,* L. H.]

Dil. [*Interposing.*] And your own——

Alice. My father—you forget——

Dil. [R.] Alice, listen to me—if not for my sake, for the sake of that father whom you profess, and truly, so affectionately to regard. He is in prison, and by whose power placed there you know—I shrink not from the avowal—it was my only chance of securing his daughter, yourself'

Alice. [L. *troubled—calling.*] Sophy! Sophy!

Dil. The housekeeper has my orders to detain her with some mild excuse, till this interview is at an end.

Alice. Oh, heaven!

Dil. Look at these securities, Alice—bills on your father to a considerable amount. He will never be able to discharge them—never! I love you fondly, devotedly—say but the word, you will be mine—sign this marriage contract, and your father is free. These bills and vouchers I instantly destroy—speak!

Alice. Cruel man! Can you look me calmly in the face, while you make so shameless a proposal?

Dil. I know it is base and infamous, Alice. I acknowledge it. But it is my only hope of success—and, in return, I offer you wealth, comfort, happiness!

Alice. Dillon! Dillon, I beseech—I implore——

Dil. Do not attempt to move me. You see, I am perfectly calm. I hope this may be the last villainy I shall commit. It rests with yourself, Alice, to render it so. There lies the contract—[*Putting it on the table.*]—sign! Your father, as I learn, is dangerously ill.

Alice, Ha! my father ill, and you detain me——

Dil. The instant that is signed, these doors are open. You shall fly to him in a carriage of your own, and instead of a damp cell, and a pallet of straw, restore him to peace, home, life! Now, then, devoted daughter, shall your father perish of want, or will you be mine!

Alice. [*Trembling Wildly.*] Come what may—give me the pen! [*Crosses to table,* R. H.] There—[*Signing.*]—there!

Dil. [*Exultingly.*] Signed! signed!

Alice. [*Starting up.*] My father—my dear father! Let me behold him once again free, happy—I care not—I care not for myself—no, no! [*Crosses to* R. H.]

Dil. Enough! the securities are in the flames! [*Burns them, off* U. E. L. H.] Now, Alice, you are mine—irrevocably mine! I swear to you that I will reform—be every thing you can wish. This day week—this day month—this day twelvemonth, if you best like, shall be the day of our nuptials. It is enough that you can only be mine—mine! [*Advancing.*] Oh, Alice—my Alice!

Alice. [*Recoiling.*] Pity! Your approach freezes my heart. I feel as if I were dying! [*Wringing her hands.*] My sister—my dear sister—where is my sister? [*Falls into chair,* R. H.]

Dil. Here!

Enter SOPHY, R. H. *with bonnet, &c,*

Sophy. Alice, what's the matter? [*To* Dillon.] What is the meaning of this? Speak!

Dil. It means, that——

Alice. [R. H. *Wildly.*] It means, Sophy, that I have sold myself, body and soul, to one that I must ever hate—despise! Read there! Alice Leslie to become the wife of Edward Dillon. His wife—ha, ha, ha! His—his! Here is wealth—here is a princely home, Sophy, for you and our poor father—and that ought to render me happy—and it will! Oh, I shall be so happy—so very happy! [*Wildly.*] But come—give me my shawl and bonnet. Let us run—let us fly to unlock the prison doors of our dear father!

Sophy. Stay—this shall not be! [*Crosses to* C.] Dillon, give me that contract—let me tear it up!

Dil. (L. H.. *Placing it in his breast*). No, no—'tis better where it is.

Sophy (c.) How dare you, sir, impose upon my sister? You think, perhaps, because our father is in prison she has no one to stand up for her. You'll find yourself mistaken.

Dil. Sophy, I have no wish to exchange words with you —at least, on this subject.

Sophy. No—because you know well enough 'tis a base, cowardly act. Oh, don't flash your eyes at me! I only wish I had a man's hand, I'd shew you one woman's heart, at least, not to be intimidated by your fury!

Alice. Dear Sophy, don't go on so. Let us away to our father—so ill, remember. Alas, should he be dead! What frightful thought comes over me? No one to close his eyes—no one! Open the door—quick—air, air! [*Calling* Father—father—'tis Alice. *Going* R. c. *she encounters* Lieutenant, *who enters, as she utters a cry of frantic joy, and sinks again into a chair.*]

Lieut. (c.) Alice!

Dil. (L.) He here! Confusion!

Lieut. My child—speak to me. Sophy, how came you in this house? What has happened to Alice?

Sophy (B. c.) Oh, father—father, you are but an instant too late. Alice has just signed a contract of marriage with that villain.

Dil. (bowing). Meaning me.

Lieut. But, sir, as I am released from prison by Mr. Bradshaw—[*Crosses* c.]—you will, I presume, have the honour to destroy that contract.

Dil. Never—never! I rather bless the good fortune which has thus providentially thrown into my hands all that my heart ever loved, yearned, or cared for. [*Gazing at* Alice.

Lieut. Villain! I came hither for the express purpose of demanding by what chance my daughters were to be found beneath your accursed roof? I ask not how this was—I now demand only the satisfaction of a gentleman, for the repeated violence heaped upon me and mine.

Dil. As you will!

Alice. Mr. Dillon! [*Crosses to* Dillon.] If you had really one spark of the love you profess for me, do, in pity, leave this room.

Dil. Willingly, Alice, at your bidding. Against your father I can bear no enmity. I go—[*Crosses to* c. *up the stage*]—remember the contract. This day month expect me! [*Exit* R. c. *bowing.*

Lieut. My poor girl! How sad and pale you look! Sold

for me ! Peace, love, all ! But it shall not be. No—I'll
return to my prison—die there, rather !

Alice and Sophy Father ?

Lieut. [*Much excited.*] Let us hasten from this lazar-
house of iniquity, while my feet have strength to move.
Strength ! That contract—that infernal compact of crime .
with innocence——

Sophy. Alas—his senses wander !

Lieut, I'll tear it—with his cruel heart—from his breast !
I am a father—with life's last gasp—I tear it—from—a—a
—fa—ther ! [*He falls, overcome by excitement*—Alice *and*
Sophy *throw themselves upon his bosom with cries of alarm
and anguish, and the Drop descends.*]

END OF ACT II.

ACT III.

SCENE I.—*A mean Apartment.* Door, L H. *A Staircase,* R, H. *A window broken, shews a lamp burning in
the street. A table, on which is needle-work, &c.*

ALICE *discovered softly descending the stairs,* R. H. *A
a lighted candle in her hand.*

Alice. [*Placing candle on table*] At length, our dear
father, worn out by excitement, sleeps. Heaven grant him
a few hours repose, while I continue my work. [*She sits.
Sighing.*] Heigho ! Buried in the vicinity of London—
concealed by the obscurity which poverty and distress sel-
dom fail to cast over their victims—we have at least es-
caped the persecution of Dillon. For myself, I could endure all—but when I think on the broken-heartedness of
my father—on the blighted youth of my poor sister, I
sink beneath the weight of this never-ending toil. [*Weeps.*]
How strange it is Sophy does not return ! She had but to
cross the street, and—[*A noise* L, H.]—ha ! I hear her—
[*Opens door,* U. E. L. H.]—come in, dear Sophy—I'm so
glad you've——

DILLON *enters* U. E. L. H. *shabbily dressed.*
Ugh ! horror ! Dillon !

Dil. Why, horror, Alice ? Is this the way you welcome
an old friend in distress ?

Alice. Distress !

Dil. Yes. Swindled, in a single night, at the gambling
table—plundered, robbed of all ! Houses, lands, horses,
furniture, all gone—all—even the Briary !

Alice. Alas, what has brought you hither?

Dil. What should, but to demand the fulfilment of our marriage contract.

Alice. Leave me! That contract is at an end.

Dil. How so?

Alice. You did not come to claim me at the appointed time.

Dil. My infernal creditors took good care of that. But I evaded them, as you did me. Mine I am resolved you shall be, Alice Leslie, and share my destiny, be it good or ill!

Alice. You seek to drive me to despair—distraction—to break my heart! Dillon—Dillon you never loved me—never! No—by violence you terrified me, and by a base unmanly stratagem compelled me to sign a contract which you, not I, have broken. Go, sir—leave this miserable abode—all—all your boasted love and cruelty have left us —and do not—do not tarry to trample on the hearts you have already crushed! [*Pointing.*] The door—go, or I summon——

Dil. A single cry of alarm—I am armed—not agains you—but the first that would lay hands upon me! [*Hurriedly.*] Why should I conceal it from you, Alice? A forgery, committed on my banker! I expect no mercy— none! Nothing is left me but flight—which you must share!

Alice. Never! Never will I quit this abode alive, the companion of a man so dissolute! Kill me—let me die here, at the feet of my poor father, whose happiness you have blighted—whose peace of mind you have wrecked! Again I almost beheld, as in a dream, that peaceful asylum of my childhood—heard there the sweet voices that memory loves—saw again my father's calm look of affection—once so bright and radiant, now, alas! how changed! [*She weeps.*]

Dil. I can delay no longer. You are mine—come!

Alice. In the name of all that is sacred leave me! My life is consecrated to the duties which I owe my unhappy father, and my unprotected sister.

Dil. Alice! Alice, it may be that I could have relinquished your beauty and fled—but your mind, Alice—your mind—a bright jewel—lies glittering in my path—I cannot pass it over, and be gone! [*Advancing.*]

Alice. [*Running to staircase.*] In yon chamber is my father. Come, then—if every beam of humanity be not extinguished in your callous breast, tear me lifeless, from his arms—for lifeless it shall be—ere, by force or inclination, I consent to see him deprived of his mind's last recognition—his age's last support!

Dil. [*Advancing.*] Mine! mine!

Sophy. [*Without,* L. H.] Alice! Alice! [Dillon *pauses.*]

Alice. Ha! Thank heaven, some one comes at last! [*Falling on her knees,*]

Dil. [*Alarmed, and retiring up,* L. H.] A footstep! should it be ——

SOPHY *runs in,* L. H. D. *pale and affrighted—a basket on her arm.*

Sophy. Alice, I'm pursued—quick, bolt the door!

Dil. [*Hastily.*] Yes, yes—bolt the door! [*Bolts it.*]

Sophy. [*Putting basket on table,* C.] Ah! who's that?

Alice. Dillon!

Sophy. [*Running to* Alice.] He here! What does he want? Oh, I comprehend—you My poor Alice, on your knees! Don't be frightened—now I'm come, I'll protect you. The man that pursued me in the street—I'm not afraid of him now I'm with you. [*Goes to window,* L. C.] He's looking up at the window—[*Calling.*]—here—here!

Dil. [L.] Silence, or I——[*Threatening.*]

Sophy. Silent! not I. Do your worst, and be hanged! then my poor sister and father would at least be rid of the terror of your presence, and that would be something worth dying for! [*Knocking,* L. H.] Ah, there he is—I'll —I will open the door, be he whoever he may! [*Advancing* L. H.]

Dil. [*Crosses to* Alice.] Then my life is in your hands, and you betray me!

Alice. No! [*Crosses to* C.] Sophy, do not open the door.

Sophy. [*Impatiently.*] Why, Alice—why?

Alice. [*Taking her hand.*] Hush! Listen to me. Yon man may be an officer of justice. [*Whispers.*]

Sophy. I hope so!

Alice. [*Drawing her from door to* C.] Hush! Hear me. Dillon has committed a crime which might draw down upon him the punishment of death.

Sophy. Death!

Alice. Let us not, Sophy—though he has wronged us, oh, how deeply!—forgot that we are the daughters of Lieutenant Leslie; and though our roof be humble, even to wretchedness, never let it be said that we violated the rights of hospitality, by betraying even an enemy to the scaffold!

Sophy. [*Proudly.*] You are right, Alice. [*Crosses* R. *to*

Dillon.] Yon door—turn to the left—it ascends to the roof of the house. [*Knocking repeated*, L. H.]

Dil. Alice ! what shall I say ?

Alice. Nothing—but fly !

Dil Thanks—thanks ! Bless you, Alice—bless you! [Dillon *crosses, and goes out*, R. H.]

Sophy. Shall I open the door now, Alice ?

Alice. No. First tell me, why did you return so terrified? I dread to hear. You lost the gold bracelet—our last re-source——

Sophy No. dear Alice. I sold it to the jeweller, as you told me, and was returning with my basket, when I found that I was watched—pursued, by——

Alice. Whom ?

Ben. [*Without.*] Ben Bradshaw

Sophy. [*Smiling.*] Oh, la! Did you hear ! As I live, it's Ben Bradshaw that I've been running away from, simple goose that I am ! mistaking him for a thief all the while. Come in, do ! [*Crossing, and going* L. H.]

Alice. Stay, Sophy—our father might not like——

Sophy. To see Ben Bradshaw ! Well, then, I should, and as father isn't here just now, it would do us good— I'm sure it would. Alice—once more to see a smile on the countenance of a friend. [*Opens* L. H. D]

Enter BEN, disguised.

Sophy and Alice. [*Recoiling.*] A stranger !

Ben. [*Untieing his throat, and laughing.*] He, he, he! 'Tis you, is it, Miss Leslie—and you, Sophy ? Why you run like a leveret. Don't you know me ?

Sophy and Alice. Ben ! [*Running to him.*]

Ben. [*Shaking their hands with great energy.*] Yes, to be sure—Ben Bradshaw—haven't changed my name—an't married—neither are you—are you, Sophy ? If you are— lor, how glad I am to have found you ! Haven't I ferretted all London—and if it hadn't been for an old acquaintance that Sophy left behind——

Sophy. [L.] I ! what old acquaintance ?

Ben. [c] This gold bracelet. [*Shewing it.*]

Alice. [R. *Blushing.*] 'Tis mine !

Ben. I know it is. Luckily. I saw it on your arm the morning brother Charles left Overhampton for Indy. Ha, ha ! let me put it there again, Miss Alice. If it hadn't been for this, I should never have found you.

Alice. How ?

Ben. Hearing you were somewhere in this neighbour-hood, I resolved to make one more effort to find you before I returned home—and as the Overhampton stage passes the street, I muffles myself up, enquiring everywhere, and looking in at shop windows till the coach passed up, when what does I clap my eyes upon but this identical bracelet. Ha, ha! says I—here's a track of the hares. So in I goes, buys the bracelet—was told the young lady as sold it had turned straight up Crooked Street. Didn't I give chase! There was Sophy! Chivey, oh—chivey, oh! says I. With that, didn't she set scampering? Didn't the people look and laugh, to see me puffing and blowing like a broken steam engine—ha, ha, ha, ha!—and an't I the happiest dog in London, to have found you once more? How's your father?

Alice. Alas, Mr. Bradshaw, much—much changed!—health, mind, well nigh lost. His misfortunes have driven him to imagine every friend a creditor—every house a prison.

Ben (looking about.) A prison! hem! I'm not much surprised at his mistaking this for one.

Sophy. [*Goes up, and sets table from basket.*] Do sit down Mr. Bradshaw, and take something—and tell us all the news from Overhampton—who's dead, who's married. Here, help me to set the table.

Ben. The best news is, that brother Charles is daily expected.

Alice (with anxiety). Charles!

Ben. Yes, and——

Lieut. (without R.) Sophy—Alice—where are my pistols? I'll shoot the villain!

Ben. Pistols— villain—who's that?

Sophy. It's father—awoke in one of his paroxysms. Don't let him see you till Alice has spoken to him—hush!

Alice. Alas, he would think——

Sophy. Never mind what he would think—Alice *crosses to* L. H.]—but just step into the crockery closet, and don't break any of our expensive china. If the coach passes I'll——

Ben. Oh, I'm in no hurry. Don't mind losing my fare. [*As she closes the door.*] She's more of a duck than ever! 'Tis she I love.

Enter LIEUTENANT *down the stairs hurriedly.*

Lieut. Where is he?

Alice. Who, dear father?

Lieut. The villain—I heard him—he's on the look out to drag me to prison again, is he? I heard him go out at the window, I tell you—there—there! [*Pointing,* R]

Alice. [*Apart to* Sophy.] Dillon !

Sophy. Dear father, there's no one in this house but friends.

Lieut. Friends ! There are no such things—no friends —none—none !

Alice. Oh, yes, dear father—you forget, when you were in trouble, Ben Bradshaw——

Lieut. Yes, yes—I forgot—yes, Ben—poor Ben—he was a solitary exception. He was very good—very good ! [Ben *peeps from closet in* F.]

Sophy. [*Coaxingly*] How pleased you would be to see him—wouldn't you, father ?

Lieut. I ? No ! [Ben *shuts door.*] Neither him nor any one else. He would only ask me for the money he lent me, and where is it to come from ? I've none—all—all gone ! [*Violently.*] I won't see anybody—I won't be intruded on by any one—I won't—I won't—duns—duns— duns ! [*Crosses to* L. *hurriedly.*]

Sophy. [*Apart—smiling.*] Poor Ben ! I wonder how long he's to remain shut up with the mice ? Plenty of 'em there !

Alice. Won't you take something to eat, dear father ?

Lieut. Supper, eh ? Can't eat—no appetite—always knocks at the door, just as one sits down. No money— can't pay—can't sleep—always noises—always—[*China crash behind,* D. F.] Ugh ! there they are again ! Give me my pistols—won't go to prison—won't ! [*Crossing to* C. D.]

Ben. [*Running out* D. F. *a broken bason in his hand.*] Pistols ! Come, I say—none of that ! [*Putting bason on his head.*]

Lieut. [*Seizing him by the collar.*] Rogue—thief—house robber—bailiff ! [*Shaking him on his knees.*]

Ben. La, Mr. Leslie—I'm no thief, nor bailiff. Look at me—I'm——

Lieut. Who—who ?

Sophy and Alice. Ben Bradshaw, father.

Lieut. [*Letting him go.*] That booby !

Ben. Booby ' Well, I never !

Lieut. Oh, what you threaten, do you ? Come to force me away from my poor girls.

Ben. No, I don't. On the contrary—I came up to town on purpose to invite you back to the Briary. It's all in apple-pie order, I can tell you.

Lieut. [*Smiling.*] The Briary ! [*Looking about despondingly.*] What place is this ? The Briary ! Aye, aye—

let's go home.—Come, girls—put on your bonnets—let's
go home.

Sophy and Alice. [*In tears—they both go to him.*]
Alas, alas!

Ben. [*Apart.*] You only humour him, as I tell you, it
will be all righ . Rely upon Ben Bradshaw. [*Coach horn
heard,* L. H] I wish I may die, if there be not the Overhampton coach—just in the nick of time. It stops ten minutes over the way—always plenty of room inside· Now,
sir, here's your hat—let's be off to the Briary.

Lieut. Aye, aye—to the Briary ! Home, home—come,
girls—come ! [*Exit with* Ben L. H. D.

Sophy and Alice. [*Calling,*] Ben—father ! What is the
meaning of this ? [*They run out after them* L. H. D.

SCENE II.—*An Hotel. Shipping, and London Bridge
by Lamplight. Lights down.*

Enter CHARLES, *from Hotel,* R. H. *with a travelling cloak
and cap on his arm.*

Charles. Now, then, to my native village, to throw myself and my newly acquired independency at the feet of
my adored Alice Leslie ! [*A noise.*] What's that ? Some
one has fallen from the window of the opposite house !

Enter DILLON, *hastily,* L H.

Are you hurt ? Shall I go for assistance ?

Dil. [*Detaining him.*] No, no— 'tis nothing ——

Charles. Ha ! Mr. Dillon !

Dil. [*Hurriedly.*] Do not betray me. I am armed, and
will not submit without a fearful struggle !

Charles. Betray you ! Don't you recognize me ? I am
Charles Bradshaw, returned from India.

Dil. Is it possible ?

Charles. Yes—and you will be happy to hear, that the
relative of my mother's, whom I went to visit, has rendered me amply rich. I am returned for the sole purpose
of offering my fortune and my heart to Alice Leslie.

Dil. [*Starting*] Alice Leslie ! [*Wrestling with pistol.*]
Does *she* love you ?

Charles. I am not without hope.

Dil. [*Apart.*] This, then, was the accursed secret of her
scorn and coldness towards me ! Ha, ha ! You'll find
Miss Leslie somewhat changed since you quitted England,
sir.

Charles. Changed ! Not married, I hope ?

Dil. Not exactly married—but her father has fallen into
poverty, and the girls are in great trouble.

Charles. [*Joyfully.*] Then I am arrived just in time, for I have plenty for all.

Dil. [*Apart—bitterly*] Hem! We shall see that! If it were not that the report of this pistol might betray me, I'd——

Voice. [*Without,* R. H.] This way—this way!

Dil. Ha! Did you come out of that hotel? [*Pointing* R. H.]

Charles. Yes.

Dil. [*Whispering.*] Were there any officers of justice inside?

Charles. Yes—in quest of some delinquent—a forger! I did not hear the poor devil's name.

Dil [*Coldly.*] 'Tis the same as mine!

Charles. [*Starting.*] Yours, Dillon?

Dil. Yes.

Charles. And the culprit——

Dil. Myself—a ruined man!

Charles. [*Troubled.*] They are searching every side of these premises. You are lost!

Dil [*Despairingly.*] I am armed——

Charles. Do not add murder to your offence. Here—take my hat and cloak—disguise yourself in them. Your look bespeaks—don't be offended with an old friend—that you want money. Take my purse, and escape in yonder boat, while I go in, and find some excuse to delay pursuit.

Voics. [*Without,* R. H.] Follow—follow—follow!

Dil. [*With emotion.*] Charles! [*Voices again heard,* R. H.]

Charles. A moment—you are lost! [*Exit hastily,* R.]

Dil. Gold! and this I owe to him—also my life—and I would—[*Playing with pistol.*]—but I am—I am a villain! [*Throws down pistol, and exit* L. H.]

———

SCENE III.—*The Briary.* [*Same as Act I. Scene III.*] *Piano, Kettle boiling, &c. Morning.*

BEN *discovered arranging furniture, breakfast table, &c.*

Ben. Fooh! There—all is now exactly as it used to be! I may put my duster into my pocket. Dear Sophy! This is her blessed song—there are her darling dogs' ears!—[*Kisses song, and sings* "He's on the sea," &c. *Looking about with approval.*] The easy chair seems to say, " Come and sit in me"—the kettle to sing, " Polly, take me off again"—and the garden, all sunshine and roses, like a true old friend, smiles in at the window, as if to welcome home the former happy companions of its blossoms and butterflies.

SOPHY *enters* L H. *dressed as at first—a bunch of flowers in her hand, from the garden.*

Sophy. What a pretty speech I heard! It only wants a little addition.

Ben. And what's that, Sophy?

Sophy. And there stands Ben Bradshaw, in the centre of all, like the good genius of the place! Oh, Ben, in what way can we possibly requite your goodness, for thus reinstating us in our old home? Only to think of your buying the cottage, and the furniture, just as it stood—the very flowers in the garden tied up by your hands!

Ben. Ah, but there is a flower, which, if I could tie up, would render me so happy!

Sophy La! Where is it?

Ben. [*Taking her hand.*] Here!

Sophy. You wouldn't tie me up, would you?

Ben. Yes—with myself, in the holy noose of matrimony. What say you, Miss Sophy—are you still engaged?

Sophy. Yes.

Ben. [*With disappointment.*] Ah! to whom?

Sophy. [*Smiling.*] To you, Ben. There's my hand, and when my poor father is better, it shall be yours for life. [*Crosses to* R. H.]

Ben. Oh—h—I shall faint! I'm not awake! Say that again, Sophy.

Sophy. When my father is better, yours for life! [*Putting flowers on chair,* R. H.]

Ben. Mine for life! I *shall* have her for a wife at last! Do give me a——

Sophy. [*Looking through the back of chair, at which she is kneeling, and sorting the flowers.*] There's heart's-ease for you.

Ben. It was *two lips* I wanted.

Sophy. [*Smiling.*] Well, take them. [*He kisses her through the back of chair.*] Be quiet—[*She rises.*]—here's Alice! [Alice *enters cautiously,* L. H.] Now, dear Alice—is father yet awake?

Alice. Yes.

Ben and Sophy. How does he seem?

Alice. At first, when he awoke, and found himself once again on his own white bed, in his own little chamber, he seemed as if the confused remembrance of a painful dream disturbed him—but a smile soon came over his features when I looked in and told him, in the usual way, that we were waiting breakfast. He got up, as formerly—dressed himself—and here he comes—looking, thank Heaven—once more like himself.

Ben. He'll become as sensible as I am yet, depend on't.

Alice (whispering). Hush—to your places, all. Now to try the effect of this generous surprise. Heaven, look on! [*Alice sits and begins to make tea—Ben dries the paper at the fire—Sophy runs to piano,* R. H., *and plays and sings ballad,* "He's on the sea," &c. *Lieutenant enters—dressed as at first—looking at them, irresolutely listening—then, with a burst of joy, he advances* L. H.]

Lieut. My children!

Sophy and Alice (running to him). Father! [*He stands for an instant in the centre of the stage, looking from one to the other, then bursts into tears. Picture*].

Lieut. I remember all now! My poor girls! [*Embraces them and weeps*].

Sophy and Alice. Dear—dear father!

Ben. (Blubbering). I must embrace something. [*Embraces them all round, hard*].

Lieut. Ah, my friend Ben—come to read the newspaper as usual. I remember you always will call it cockswain, when you know its coxen!

Ben. I wish he'd remember the breakfast! The rolls will be all spoiled. Let me place your chair, sir. [*Gets behind,* L. H. *A knock at door,* L. H.]

Lieut. Come in!

Enter CHARLES, L. H. D.

Ben. Hang me, if it be not brother Charles, just in time for our wedding! [*Apart to* Sophy—*down* R.]

Alice. Charles!

Charles (running to her). Dearest Alice!

Ben. Oho! just in time for his own wedding, too!

Sophy (aside—whispers) Don't you remember the bracelet?

Ben. Hem! I'm awake!

Alice. The sudden surprise—Charles returned!

Charles. Yes, Alice—returned affluent beyond my hopes. Wealth, which only renders me happiness confirmed by you.

Ben. Come, I say, that's not so bad. But can't we eat and talk? [*All go up and sit.*] Mercy on me, Charles—why your complexion looks like India rubber! Mother won't own you! Do wipe your face. Oh, I forgot, that's the duster!

DILLON, *disguised as a* Gipsy Pedlar, *passes window,* L. C

Dil. (without). Knives! scissors!

Lieut. [*Calling*] No. no, my good friend—go your ways.

Ben. Scissors, indeed' [*Sings.*] "Scissors cut as well knives!" and quite un——

Dil. [*Without*] Wedding rings! wedding rings!

Ben. [*Rising.*] Wedding rings! Oh, that's quite another affair! Come in! [*Opens* L. H. D. DILLON *enters.*] Where are them wedding rings you spoke of? Oh, here they are!

Dil. [*Taking paper from box.*] Here is also a wedding contract!

Ben. A what?

Alice. [*Trembling.*] That voice!

Dil. A contract of marriage, between Edward Dillon and Alice Leslie! [*All rise* Ben *gets round to* R. H.]

Charles. How!

Dil. Read, sir—read——

Charles. [*With anxiety,*] Did you sign that, Alice?

Alice. [*Trembling.*] I did!

Lieut. [*Advancing.*] That demon here again! Let me—

Dil. Stay! I only beg to be heard a few words, then call me what you please. No one needs fear a branded man, and I am he! A few brief hours must conduct me either to exile or the scaffold—then, listen to me—you, most of all, Alice Leslie—since it is to do an act of justice, and to implore your forgiveness that I am here.

Alice. My forgiveness!

Dil. It will not be denied. Alice—Alice! I that have loved you so long, and hopelessly, now know your secret —yes—another last night, inadvertently, betrayed an affection for you, which I felt to be returned. Oh, heaven! what jealous maddening phrenzy flashed across my despairing heart! My hand wrestled with the cold steel, and I was about to become the murderer of Charles Bradshaw!

Charles. Of me, Dillon?

Dil. Yes. A moment, and this frantic hand had plunged you, as a detested rival, into eternity, when the voices o my pursuers arrested my arm. and you, for the death I intended you, gave me life. Hunted from place to place, a change has come over me I am an altered man, Alice— I have repented—prayed—and. as a last atonement, bring you back this contract. and bid yoo farewell for ever! [*Tears, and gives contract.*] Under safe convoy to a distant land I go. Alice, I gaze on you but this once— do not—do not quite curse the memory of one, who, with all his mistaken faults, loved you even to madness! Tears! tears! [*Kissing her hand.*] God bless you, Alice! I go—

to die! [*Rushes out* L. H. D. *and passes window—a moment of consternation,*]

Lieut Come, come, my girls—no tears. This is but the every-day example, where self-will is permitted to become a man's rock-a-head. Teach your children better—teach them early, and heaven will bless them, my girls, as I do you!

Ben. He's gone—and I haven't paid him for the wedding ring!

Sophy. Pay him when he calls again!

Ben. I wonder whether this would fit?

Sophy. [*Putting out her finger.*] Try!

Ben. [*Putting it on.*] Fits exactly! I feel myself married already! Won't we have a flare up at the Briary? Open doors—invite every body! And I hope our friends will come often—very, very often, to welcome Ben Bradshaw, and his dear little wife, " HOME AGAIN."

THE CURTAIN FALLS.

MUSIC OF BURLESQUES, OPERAS, AND DRAMAS TO LOAN.

NOTE.—Piano and vocal parts are marked p. v. The figures in columns denote the PRICE per MONTH.—DEPOSIT: TWO MONTHS' HIRE.

	s.	d.
Acis and Galatea, burl. p. v. ...10		6
Agreeable Surprise, opera, p. v. ... 2		6
Aladdin, opera 5		0
Aladdin, [Miss Keating] burl. p. v. 2		6
Aladdin, Byron, burl. p. v... ...20		0
Ditto, 8 band parts 15		0
Alcestis, burl. p. v. 10		6
Ali Baba [Miss Keating] burl. p. v. 5		0
Ali Baba [Byron] burl. p. v. ...20		0
Ditto, 8 band parts 15		0
All at C, p. v. 15		0
Alonzo the Brave, burl. p. v. ...20		0
Ditto, 9 band parts 15		0
Ashore and Afloat, drama, 10 band		
parts... ...10		0
Atalanta, burl., 5 band parts .. 7		6
Bare-faced Imposters, farce, p. v.... 5		0
Beauty and Beast [Keating] p. v.... 5		0
Beggars' Opera, vocal score ... 3		6
Black Beard, opera, p. v. 3		6
Black Eyed Susan, drama, full score 5		0
Black Eyed Susan, burl. p. v. ...20		0
Ditto, 9 band parts 20		0
Blind Boy, opera, p. v. ... 3		6
Blue Beard, drama, p. v. 5		0
Blue Beard Repaired, p. v.... ...30		0
Blue Beard [Byron's] burl. p. v. ...15		0
Ditto, 6 band parts 10		0
Blue Beard [Miss Keating] p. v. ... 6		0
Bombastes, p. v. 7		6
Ditto, 6 band parts 5		0
Bronze Horse, drama, p. v.... ...20		0
Brown and the Brahmins, burl. p. v.15		0
Brother and Sister, opera, p. v. ... 5		0
Bottle Imp, drama, 1 & 2 violin, basso 3		0
Cabinet, opera, p v 3		0
Camaralzaman, extrav. p v ..15		0
Camp, The, opera, p v 2		6
Cast King of Granada, extrav., p v10		0
Castle Grim [Reece] comic op. p v 5		0
Castle of Andalusia, opera, p v ... 3		6
Castle Spectre, opera, p v 2		6
Cataract of Ganges, dra. 6 band pts10		0
Charles XII, instrumental of song,		
"Rise, Gentle Moon" 3		6
Children in the Wood, opera, p v... 2		6
Ching Chang Fou, burl. p v ...10		0
Cinderella [Byron] burl. 8 band pts 15		0
Cinderella [Byron] burl. p v ...20		0
Cinderella [Miss Keating] burl. p v 5		0
Cinderella, opera, p v 7		6
Clari, opera, p v 7		6
Comus, opera, p v 5		0
Court of Lyons, burl. p v ...15		0
Cricket on Hearth, dra. 10 bnd pts 5		0
Critic, opera, p v 2		6
Daughter of Danube, extra. v 4 band		
parts.. 5		0
Dearer than Life, drama, 9 band pts 10		6
Deeds not Words, drama, 11 band		
parts... 7		6

	s.	d.
Devil's Bridge, opera, p v 7		6
Dolly, comic opera, p v 15		0
Ditto, 14 band parts 15		0
Don Cæsar de Bazan, drama, p v... 7		6
Don Juan, pant., 4 band parts ... 3		6
Dreamland, cantata, p v 10		0
Duenna, opera, p v 3		6
Duke's Motto, drama, 9 band parts 15		0
Eddystone Elf, drama, 6 band parts 5		0
Ernani, burl., 9 band parts ...10		0
Esmeralda, burl., p v... ... 5		0
Ditto, 10 band parts 15		0
Exile, opera, p v 3		6
Fair Helen, opera, p v 7		6
Fair Rosamond's Bower, burl., p v 10		0
Fairyland, fairy play, p v 7		6
False Alarms [Braham] opera, p v 2		6
False Alarms [King] opera, p v ... 3		6
Fanchette, speretta, p v 5		0
Farmer, opera, p v 3		6
Farmer, opera, p v 2		6
Father and Son, drama, 5 band pts 5		0
Field of Cloth of Gold, burl., p v...20		0
Forest of Bondy, opera, p v ... 5		0
Fortunio, extrav., 9 band parts ...15		0
Forty Thieves, opera, p v 2		6
Fra Diavola, burl., p v ...20		0
Ditto, 9 band parts 15		0
Frankenstein, burl. 6 band parts ... 5		6
Frederick the Great, opera, p v ... 4		0
Ganem, vocal, 13 band parts ...15		0
Geraldine, p v... 10		0
Golden Fleece, song, "I'm still		
flutter," p v 1		0
Graziella, cantata, p v 10		0
Guy Mannering, drama, p v ...10		0
Ditto, 6 band parts 5		0
Happy Man, p v... 3		6
Ditto, 10 band parts 7		6
Hamlet, grave-digger's song and		
accom. 1		0
Hartford Bridge, opera, p v .. 2		6
Harvest Home. pastoral cantata p v 10		0
Haunted Mill, p v 3		6
Haunted Tower, comic opera, p v 5		0
Haunted Tower, opera, p v ... 2		6
He would be an Actor, full score .. 2		6
Highland Lassie Ballet, 3 band pts. 3		6
Highland Reel, opera, p v ... 2		6
High Life below Stairs, song, "All		
in a Livery" 1		0
House that Jack Built, full score 10		0
Ill-treated Trovatore, p. v.........15		0
Ditto, 9 band parts 15		0
Illustrious Stranger, p. v. ... 5		0
Invincible, The, opera, p. v. ... 5		6
Ivanhoe, burl. p. v.................15		0
Ditto, 8 band parts............10		0
Ixion, p. v. 20		0
Ditto, 9 band parts 15		0

Title	s.	d.
Jack Sheppard (songs in)	1	0
Jeanette's Wedding, p. v.	15	0
Jean of Arc, burl. p. v.	15	0
Jean of Arc, drama, 4 band parts	5	0
Kenilworth, burl. p. v.	20	0
King Alfred and the cakes, burl.p.v.	3	0
Lady Godiva, vocal, and 13 band pts.	20	0
Lady of Lyons, [Byron] burl. p. v.	15	0
Ditto, 5 band parts	10	0
La Somnambula [Byron] burl.	15	0
Ditto. 6 band parts	10	0
Little Red Riding Hood, p. v.	7	6
Loan of a Lover, p. v.	5	0
Lock and Key, opera, p. v.	2	6
Lodoiska, opera, p. v.	2	6
Lord Lovel, p. v.	7	6
Lost and Found	5	0
Love in a Village, p. v.	5	0
Love in a Village, opera, p. v.	3	6
Love's Limit, comic opera, p. v.	7	6
Luke the Labourer, 6 band parts	2	6
Macbeth, tragedy, v. score & 8 b. pts.	19	0
Macbeth Travestie, p. v.	7	6
Ditto, 4 band parts	5	0
Madame Angot, p. v.	5	0
Maid and Magpie, drama, p. score	3	6
Maid and Magpie, [Byron] burl. p.v.	20	0
Ditto, 9 band parts	15	0
Maid of Mill, opera, p.v.	5	0
Maid of the Mill, opera, p. v.	2	6
Maid with Milking Pail (song)	1	0
Manager Strutt, 8 band parts	5	0
Mariner's Compass, drama, 11 b. p.	15	0
Marriage by Lantern Light, p. v.	5	0
Marriage Figaro, C'tess pt, with bass	5	0
Mary Turner, p. v.	10	0
Ditto, 12 band parts	15	0
Masaniello, burl. p. v.	20	0
Masaniello, drama, 4 band parts	3	6
Masaniello, opera, p. v.	10	0
Matrimony, opera, p. v.	3	6
Mazeppa, burl. p. v.	20	0
Ditto, 10 band parts	10	0
Medea, burl. full vocal score	10	0
Ditto, 8 band parts	10	0
Merchant of Venice(unpub.songs of)	2	0
Midas, p. v.	5	0
Mids. Night's Dream, [Bishop] p. v.	7	6
Military Billy Taylor, p.v.	15	0
Miller and Men, burl. p. v.	10	0
Ditto. 9 band parts	10	0
Miller and Men, drama, 5 band parts	7	6
Miller and his Men, opera, p. v.	5	0
Miller Out-witted, 3 band parts	2	6
Minerali, 3 band parts	2	6
Mischief-Making, vocal & 13 b. pts	10	0
Monsieur Jacques, p. v.	5	0
Mother Goose, harl., orig, p. v.	5	0
Motto, burl., p. v.	10	0
Motto, burl. 9 band parts	15	0
My Grandmother, opera, p. v.	2	0
My Poll and my Partner Joe, burl.p.v.	15	0
No, 4 band parts	2	6
No Song, no Supper, opera, p. v.	5	0
Nurseryrymia, Fairy play, p. v.	5	0
Of Age to-morrow, opera	3	6
Orpheus and Eurydice, [Brough]p.v.	2	6
Padlock, The, opera, p. v.	3	6
Pas de Fascination, 8 band parts	5	0
Patient Penelope, p. v.	10	0
Paul and Virginia, opera, p. v.	3	0
Peeping Tom of Coventry, opera,p.v.	3	6
Perdita, burl. p. v.	20	0
Pet Dove [Gounod] com. op. full v.sc.	5	0
Pirates, opera, p.v.	5	0
Pizarro, p. v.	3	0
Ditto, 4 band parts	2	0
Poor Soldier, opera, p. v.	2	6
Prize, The, opera, p. v.	2	6
Purse, The, opera	2	6
Puss in Boots, [Planché] full score	7	6
Puss in Roots [Miss Keating] p. v.	5	0
Quaker, p. v.	5	0
Raymond and Agnes, 3 band parts	3	0
Raymond and Agnes, opera, p. v.	7	6
Rob Roy, p. v.	5	0
Ditto, 9 band parts	5	0
Robin Hood, burl. p. v.	15	0
Ditto, 9 band parts	15	0
Robinson Crusoe, p. v.	5	0
Review, p. v.	5	0
Robert Macaire, 4 band parts	2	6
Rosina, opera, p. v.	3	6
Sentinel, p. v.	5	0
Ditto, 14 band parts	15	0
Sleeping Beauty [Miss Keating] p.v.	5	0
Signor Pantaloon, p. v.	20	0
Swiss Swains, v, sc. opening chorus	5	0
Sister's Sacrifice, 11 band parts	15	6
Sweethearts and Wives, p. v.	5	6
Swiss Cottage, p. v.	5	0
Ditto, 6 band parts	5	6
Slave, The, opera, p. v.	5	0
Son-in-law, opera, p.v.	3	6
St. David's Day, opera, p.v.	3	6
Siege of Belgrade, opera, p. v.	2	6
Shepherd of Cournouilles, p. v.	3	6
Sardanapalus, tragedy, entire music	7	6
Trombalcazar, p. v.	7	6
Trooper's Horn, full score	7	6
Tell with a vengeance, p. v.	7	6
Ditto, 10 band parts	7	6
Tale of Mystery, opera, p. v.	3	0
Timour the Tartar, opera, p. v.	4	6
Turnpike Gate, opera, p. v.	3	6
Three and the Deuce, opera, p.v.	2	6
Vilikins and Dinah, p. v.	7	6
Vampire, 4 band parts	5	0
Watch and Wait, drama, 8 bnd prts	7	6
White Horse of Peppers, p. v.	2	6
Ditto, 6 band parts	2	6
William Tell [Brough] p.v.	2	6
White Cat [Keating] p. v.	3	0
White Cat [Planché] full score	5	0
Whittington and Cat, 7 band parts	5	0
Welsh Girl, overture, full score	2	6
Willow Pattern Plate, 9 band parts	7	6
Wallace, Hero of Scotl'd, opera, p.v.	3	6
Waterman, p. v.	2	6
Who's the Heir, operetta, p. v.	4	0
Who stole the clock, opera bouffe,p.v.	7	6
Wedding Day, opera, p. v.	5	0
Widows Bewitched, operetta p. v.	10	0
Windsor Cstl.[Burnand]op.burl.p.v.	2	6
Yellow Dwarf [Miss Keating] p. v.	3	0

INTERNATIONAL
DESCRIPTIVE CATALOGUE

OF

PLAYS,

AND

DRAMATIC WORKS.

◆

CONTENTS.

COPIES OF ANYTHING IN THIS CATALOGUE SENT FREE OF POSTAGE IN
GREAT BRITAIN ON RECEIPT OF PRICE. FOREIGN POSTAGE
MUST BE ADDED.

*In ordering and remitting by Mail always send Post Office
Orders if possible.*

LONDON.

SAMUEL FRENCH,

PUBLISHER,

89, STRAND.

NEW YORK:

SAMUEL FRENCH & SON,

PUBLISHERS,

122, NASSAU STREET.

Payment MUST accompany each Order.

FRENCH'S ACTING EDITION—7s. per Vol., 6d. each.

FRENCH'S ACTING EDITION
(Late LACY'S).

SYLVESTER
DAGGERWOOD.

LONDON:
SAMUEL FRENCH,
PUBLISHER,
89, STRAND.

NEW YORK:
SAMUEL FRENCH & SON,
PUBLISHERS,
122, NASSAU STREET.

ABERDEEN—
WM. RUSSEL, 19, Broad Street.
BATH—S. J. COOK, The Civet Cat,
4, Abbey Churchyard.
BELFAST—
JAMES MOORE, Cheapside.
BIRMINGHAM—
J. GUEST, 52, Bull Street.
BRADFORD—
WM. MORGAN, 31, Kirkgate.
BRISTOL—
E. TOLEMAN, 2, Rupert Street.
CORK—
W. J. MURRAY, 90, George's St.
DUBLIN—
J. WISEHEART, 23, Suffolk Street.
EDINBURGH—
H. ROBINSON, 11, Greenside Street.
GLASGOW—
WM. LOVE, 226, Argyle Street.
LEEDS—
G. RAMSDEN, 13, Vicar Lane.
LIVERPOOL—
F. R. WILKINS, 22, Christian St.
MANCHESTER—
JOHN HEYWOOD, 143, Deansgate.

NEWCASTLE-ON-TYNE—
THOMAS ALLEN, 36, Collingwood St.
PLYMOUTH—
A. BURNELL, 2, Mount Pleasant.
PORTSMOUTH—
BURROWS & Co., 97, High Street.
SHEFFIELD—
GEO. SLATER, 54, Snighill.
PARIS—
J. G. FOTHERINGHAM,
8, Rue Neuve-des-Capucines
BOMBAY—
THACKER, VINING & Co.
CALCUTTA—
THACKER, SPINK AND Co.
CANADA—
BUTLAND, Toronto.
MELBOURNE—
CHARLWOOD, 7, Bourke Street, E.
C. MUSKETT, 78, Bourke Street, E.
NEW ZEALAND—
J. BRAITHWAITE, Dunedin.
W. M. STANTON, Nelson.
SYDNEY—
F. KIRBY, 228, Pitt St.

(By order) of all Booksellers in England and Colonies.
NEW DESCRIPTIVE CATALOGUE SENT POST FREE.

NO BOOKS EXCHANGED.

www.ingramcontent.com/pod-product-compliance
Lightning Source LLC
Chambersburg PA
CBHW081305040426
42452CB00014B/2658